HOW TO USE THIS BOOK

All children love to look at bright,
colourful pictures and picture
recognition is an important part of the
learning process.
Go over each page with your child,
point to the picture, and name the object
shown. Then ask your child to repeat the
name of the object.

baby's first picture book

illustrated by Ken McKie

cup

dish

spoon

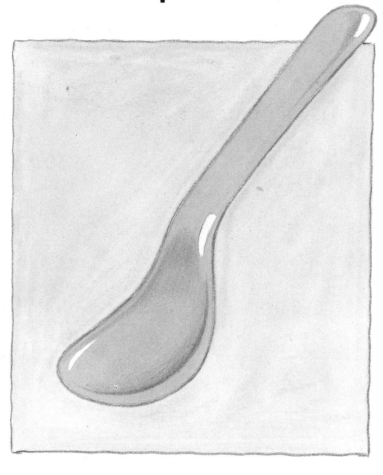

chair

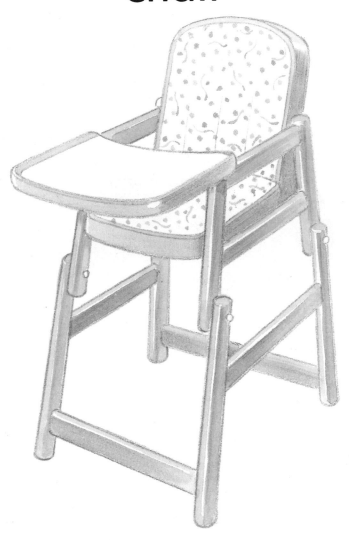

apple

banana

brush

comb

doll

bricks

shoes

socks

coat

hat

mittens

buggy

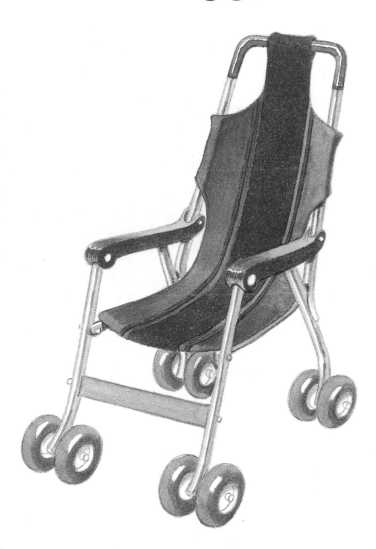

ball

baby

rabbit

car

bath

toothbrush

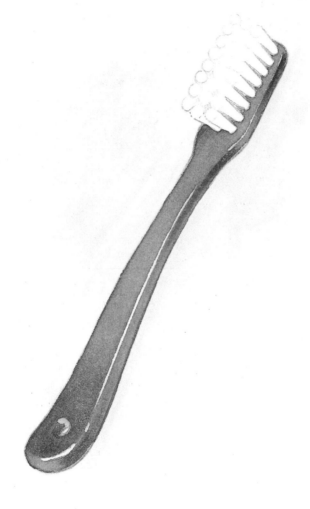

pyjamas

teddy